POWER THOUGHTS 4 CHRISTIANS

15 KEYS 4 A REVITALISED LIFE IN CHRIST

BY CALLUM COKER

© 2025 Callum Coker. All rights reserved.

ISBN 978-1-991359-39-1

Paperback.

First International Trade edition: February 2025.

A CIP catalogue record for this book is available from the National Library of New Zealand.

No part of this publication may be reproduced, stored in a retrieval system, transmitted in any form or by any means without the written permission of the author. The only exception is brief quotations.

OTHER BOOKS BY CALLUM COKER

THE FREEDOM MESSAGE: PSALMS

THE FREEDOM MESSAGE: PROVERBS

THE FREEDOM MESSAGE: ECCLESIASTES

THE FREEDOM MESSAGE: GALATIANS

THE FREEDOM MESSAGE: EPHESIANS

THE FREEDOM MESSAGE: PHILIPPIANS

THE FREEDOM MESSAGE: COLOSSIANS

THE FREEDOM MESSAGE: AMOS

THE FREEDOM MESSAGE: MALACHI

THE FREEDOM MESSAGE: GALATIANS +

FREEDOM POINTS

THE FREEDOM MESSAGE: PSALMS LARGE

PRINT EDITION

THE FREEDOM MESSAGE: PROVERBS LARGE

PRINT EDITION

THE PURPOSE OF LIFE

BIBLICAL MEDITATION & DEVOTIONAL 4

FEBRUARY: 28 DAYS OF GOD'S ABIDING

PRESENCE

Chapter 1

Create a vision with God

Having clear vision is vital to success. God wants us to see clearly and to line up our words with truth. He does not want us to be double minded but to see clearly, hear clearly and shape the world around us with his grace that empowers. This is the vital truth that we must live out of to experience success. Success without God in the picture is a delusion, it carries no hope. No Jesus in the picture = a lot of rat-wheel living with no forward momentum to experience breakthrough and success.

God wants to chisel away bad habits and restore blessing at every turn. Jesus doesn't want you to suffer in silence, he's active, fully engaged and ready to destroy idols at every turn. God is freedom, God is love. Freedom without a fight is luxury. Jesus didn't call us to luxury, he called us to bring heaven to earthnot to solemnly wait to get there. Understanding is breathed after knowledge, but revelation is found in the fields of love and intimacy with the Father, Son and Holy Spirit. It's a love relationship he is after, a powerful connection that is built on time spent with him. You can be at work, in the garden and still be in a posture of intimacy with God. There is no separation in the realm of the spirit and the natural realm. they are both the Lord's creation and he sees both through a lens of passionate love. The two are married together, it is a beautiful thing. God wants us to be full of his presence. Presence in a believers life is a well dug from the hard yards spent in fellowship with the giver and sustainer of life.

Jesus builds with humility and intimacy. These are sure and real, they do not change in their effectiveness for breakthrough. It's in this context that the Lord does mighty work.

Chapter 2

Develop spiritual intelligence

Knowledge is good but it isn't the pinnacle on our quest for spiritual intelligence. Spiritual intelligence is not taught in schools but it is a life drenched in the scriptures and a fulfilling connection with Jesus.

There is no hope without sacrifice and time spent developing your spiritual intelligence is not time wasted at all. It is worthy and develops significant spiritual muscle. Muscle atrophies if you don't use it consistently, our prayer, praise and reading Gods word muscles need to be exercised daily, they are that important on our mission to bring down an evil dictatorial and cruel devil who is still active in the world but ultimately impotent due to Jesus victory on the cross. Out of the strong foundation of intimacy with Christ through the three practices of biblical reading, praise and prayer comes the generosity of serving.

Generosity is a catalyst for change in the Christian life but it only carries real punch and power out of a rich treasure house within the context of a precious and rich relationship with Jesus Christ. He really is that good, it is that simple. Get to know him and live from his love. Although there have been distractions and distortions to the grace message within the church and from wolves who seek harm within the body of Christ, there is a truth that is undeniable, Grace is the unmerited, unearned, undeserved favour of God.

Don't stop pressing forward in the midst of chaos, God is for us and he loves it when we face challenges with a resolute focus that is completely set on his ways. He doesn't want us caught up in frivolous agenda but his beauty and splendour. So, lift up Jesus who is the author and finisher of our faith. There is no chaos in his paradigm of love. He is orderly, neat, tidy and resplendent. The sun rises on time each day. The skies open on time and with joy. Ordering your life according to his governance and timing is beauty and splendour.

Chapter 3

Keep God first place in your life

When we put Christ first in our own lives we are in essence rightly dividing the novel in our own lives. What do I mean by this? Simply put: The Bible is all about Jesus. When you see Jesus in the scriptures you are correctly seeing Jesus. Don't stop feeding on truth, when we first come to Christ it is all about him but over time we can become despondent and slink back into routine. Our choice to be in love with Jesus is precisely that: A choice. Our mission is secondary to Gods leading. That has to be the primary focus. Without his love leading us we are merely a gong that has no life. Walking in his will is our number one priority. His will and direction is life at its very best. It is our authentic compass point. It is the byproduct of a lifestyle of the believer that loves and treasures his presence above all else. He loves us in spite of our mistakes. Jesus has built love and grace into his message living from his fountains of truth is experiencing life at its very best. Each denomination is a brushstroke in God's masterpiece a - part of Gods family. Keeping God first place means taking the time to be in God's family and be nourished in his presence amongst the family of Christian believers that he has called you to be a part of and serve. God's heart is for unity not division. He wants us all to catch 'da-vision.' - not division. If we can see as God sees, carry hope into the everyday seemingly mundane parts of our lives we can be transformers for his glory. Our lives are to be anchored and fixed to God's promises. God's promises keep us solid, fixed on the strategies of heaven. If we long for his word we long for his best.

As we gather his truth into our hearts, he begins to move closer, then we can dine with him through the vicissitudes of this life. Dining with Christ is bliss. Doing it all by yourself is a waste of time and energy.

Chapter 4

You have a team with you

We need a team around us. This team formed when the time of A.D. came into existence. God's promises are for all time and he has led us to a dynamic people group called the church, these people are Christians and they make up his bride the church, a powerful and anointed team to destroy the powers of darkness.

Discovering treasure in God is a collective assignment not an isolated case of misunderstanding and doubt. Doubt is not a friend of faith but it is a question you can gladly take to the Holy Spirit. To bring solutions, to tackle grievances and to be all that you are called to be. God wants you, all of you so that means your fears, doubts, trepidations and concerns he wants to be a partner of and work through them one by one, breaking down that turf of doubt with his light, armour and glory.

God is militant against darkness. He wants us free in all seasons, unshackled from fear and radiating his glory. God wants to be let loose and to beautify our surroundings. Will you let him? Will I let him? This is the challenge we are faced with, contend or submit, enlarge your vision or slink back into mediocrity.

Being a part of Christian community is then essential to the overcoming life in Christ, we need to think different to the world's ways and that means having an interdependent mindset that leans on the gifts and strengths of others in the body of Christ, if we are off doing our own thing the whole time we can't be effective in the ministry that God has called us too. We need each other and we need God but we cannot have each other before God. Our relationship to Christ must be first place. That is not up for debate in the believers manual for life. Christ first but then out of that overflow we can love others.

Chapter 5

Good triumphs over evil

The forces of good will always triumph in the end against the forces of darkness. God is not socialist, republican, right wing or democrat, he is love, his judgments are perfect, he alone raises up Kings and Queens. He is the author and finisher of our faith. We all need to step out of our comfort zone occasionally. It's not okay to let gifts lie dormant and sit on the sidelines and its not okay to be hopeless when he has released so much hope to us in the form of his son and his permanent victory over sin and death.

We have to activate truth within the depths of our being. It is vital that as believers we anchor our motives and intentions in truth and not wishful philosophy that has no true north. Releasing grace was worth the risk for Jesus. it is worth exploring and being completely invested in a lifestyle of God's love and grace. As we shelter ourselves in God's healing presence.

Christ invites you to be enveloped and cocooned in his love. Jesus is so much better than you could ever hope for or imagine. The scriptures can't contain him but they do reveal him, he's bigger than the words of scripture but his words reveal his heart to build, bless and heal but also rebuke those who have gone off the narrow road of closeness, shelter and adventure with him.

When you live in his love all of heaven takes note. When you are set on the status quo, Satan is primed and ready to attack. When you are advancing forward, there is opposition but there is also hope. A life of luxury is not fulfilling without deep wells of internal investment in our spiritual development through prayer. We have to cultivate deep alliances with the Holy Spirit and the word of God to be catapulted into brand new fresh dimensions of God's grace so we can experience God's best. Grace is the propelling of our hearts into the fullness of God. A life lived in Christ is beauty, wholeness, victory and delight, it is never dull, obtuse or boring it is festive, brilliant and decadent.

The more we immerse ourselves in his truth the more we can overcome the obstacles that are in-front of us. They look like ice-burgs to the Titanic, but they are building blocks and stepping stones to other people who want to change the landscape with God's goodness. We need Jesus. We need hope but more than that we need to be full of Christ and become fully invested in his plans and purpose.

When heaven connects with our hearts, things happen, really good things happen. When we are in his love there isn't really much else that matters. A person in love, thinks about the welfare of others, they care, they are immersed, they blossom wherever they are planted. For our world to look different, we have to make a strong stand for truth. We have to allow his truth to immerse our being in love. The truth sets us free but without love it has a direct correlation to a religious spirit.

We can't neglect our inner life in pursuit of outer decorative pursuits. It's in Christ where victories are found. He brings momentum to our pursuits and authenticity is fully expressed.

Jesus is not interested in half-hearted pursuit. He is fully absorbed in taking our hearts into fresh and new territory that cannot be captured by the enemy under any set of circumstances.

The more we spend time with Jesus, the less we are interested in the distractions of the world. All that glitters is not gold. The world has so many choices and distractions to dish up and deliver. Jesus is all consuming of our struggles and he is purposeful in changing us into new people. He is love and he doesn't leave us helpless, he gives us himself so that we can become new creations. Christ is the ultimate in truth.

Chapter 6

Pursue truth & freedom at any cost

Continuing to shine the light of truth regardless of cost is freedom, this is life at its very best. Grace is kingdom living but unconnected to truth, grace is destructive, it can give way to the false concept of hyper grace that has hurt a plethora of churches and human hearts. God is good, extremely good but we need his love, we need his goodness. Grace is the force that leads humanity into wholeness and the saviours delight. Grace brings treasured morsels of delight in the daily rhythms of the mundane. It is goodness, wholeness and well-being for all. We can't become lethargic in our faith when we are living in partnership with the Holy Spirit and living from his grace.

We need to continually purpose ourselves in his presence and reawaken our passions in his incredible presence. There is no limit to his goodness but there are very real limits to our lives if we choose to reject this love and wisdom. His beauty is expressed in our lives when we turn to him and make him first place. God is extremely good. He is a God who blesses. It is in his nature to be awesome 100% of the time but we have to purpose ourselves in his love. Become committed to his purposes and forget our former patterns of living that completely contradict his love and purposes. Jesus is not going to approve sin. He is not in the business of passively approving abhorrent lifestyles that contradict his word.

Never get tired of doing the right thing. The right thing done well with a heart full of love breeds hope and secures your destiny and future in Christ. Hope and truth are always a wonderful way to conduct your life. Jesus chose us and when we dine together with Jesus there is synchronicity and timing that will marvel the public. Jesus is constantly looking to take spaces in the deeper recesses of our hearts. He is on a military offensive to capture more and more territory of our hearts, minds and careers. There is not a single component of our lives that he isn't after. All of us were designed to be immersed in his goodness.

His love and goodness is the way forward, not judgment and hate devoid of context. Where judgement is rife it is certain that a religious spirit is close by wreaking havoc and luring people away from the grace message of Christianity.

Authentic Christianity is life immersed and committed to his presence, timing and word. Ecclesiastes says 'there is a time' for everything. If you move aggressively against his will you can expect roadblocks, significant road blocks. The rhythm of love is one of awe and expectancy. He activates hope drenched in his goodness. Love without Jesus is amputated from its true and lasting source. Only life in Christ has its full meaning and definition. Jesus is the only pathway to true meaning. A life committed to his principles and presence is joy everlasting.

Chapter 7

Beware of competing gods

Idols are often sneaky, you don't often go after them they tend to find you through your inherited Spiritual D.N.A, ideas and concepts that captivate your heart and compete with the kingdom of God that have been passed down for generations that are an abomination to the mind and heart of God, Yahweh the true and living God.

The old testament idols were a lot different to the ones we have today but they are still the same in their goal and intention to take hearts and minds away from serving God. If Satan can't have our hearts, he will attempt to pull us away through distractions.

Being vigilant of your time and your space is therefore crucial in developing a heart that rests in the freedom of the cross and lives from the victory of Christ's resurrection.

I have found in my own life that if I do not pay attention to what is happening infront of me and am not pursuing God wholeheartedly I am actually opening up a door to the enemy in my life. I have to stay vigilant against the traps and schemes of Satan and understand how he operates. He wants our minds, he wants our hearts and he wants us out of heaven and not releasing the thoughts, sounds and imaginations from the heavenly realm. These are some of his main goals.

Chapter 8

All Logic is founded in God's word

Logic without definition is a senseless base for all stupidity. It's cruel to not immerse yourselves in God's presence and then expect him to bless you whenever he flippantly desires. God is a rewarder of those who choose to be with him and align their will with his beauty and wisdom. His magnificence is clearly beyond comparison but one must spend time getting to know him to hear his voice and be privy to the sounds and discussions of heaven.

There has to be a breaking away from the world's ideas, there has to be a resolute pursuit of his best, A fresh pathway out of the wilderness into new horizons. Jesus longs for us to have a meaningful existence that leaves a legacy and advances the kingdom of God here on earth. That is life at its very best. A life full of Jesus that rejects the devil and his minions. It tackles sin issues without fear and drives away demons with vigilance.

We are pearls among swine as believers, we carry truth as a barometer for our decision making and we don't ever seek to partner with Satan's troops as they press forward. Campaigning for change and being the change are two different things. Campaigning is based on hope. Making it your lifestyle to personify grace and wisdom are the truths that anchor us to hope.

Authentic beauty is a person and that person is Jesus. Beauty is inward in the Kingdom it is outward in the world. Life is inward in the Kingdom it is outward from the world's lens. When you reject the person of Jesus, you get all sorts of alternatives thrown at you by the world.

There are no life-giving alternatives to Jesus, none. We need to be traversing right to the heart of matters and begin to address the core needs of our hearts with Jesus and the Holy Spirit's tender wisdom anchoring this vast territory of exploration.

Chapter 9

Let the Holy Spirit reign supreme with God's word

We push back against enemy fortresses when the dove of the Holy Spirit is given permission to roam freely and to dress your life with clean clothes. Your to-do lists will be done lists when the King of King's cutting-edge revelation begins to saturate your minds with wisdom. It is cultivated in the secret place and lived out in the open spaces of our lives. Jesus is going to make friends with those who go after him in solitude and live out his reality in the day to day. There is always space to pursue God, always.

You can make time for him and transform your existence. You are not trapped in the day to day. Fresh rhythms of his grace are poured out daily. There is no denying his goodness when we are walking closely with him feasting on promises. Being filled with new hope is a decision, a posture, a joy that the dedicated believer can experience and live from permanently. God is not going to anchor his beloved bride in mediocrity when we were called to be world changers to propel nations into their destinies, into their purpose. God came for full victory in all areas not isolated successes distant from his will and timing. Blessing is found in his word and lined out day to day with him flowing into our daily encounters.

When his blessing is poured out so too is his love. Prosperity is not a dirty word to the Lord it is a sign of his favour. If you tithe, give and are generous for kingdom exploits then God can propel you forward in a mighty way with kingdom principles. Nothing truly good can be found outside of his will that is why it is crucial to be in love, to be in partnership with him and not aloof doing your own thing. The secret place of God is a gateway to wisdom because truth is being cultivated and nourished through biblical patterns of intimacy. Intimacy with Christ is the gateway to wisdom.

God is magnificent. Jesus is not absent in our difficulties. He is in fact, supreme and in charge - sovereign is the technical term that theologians deploy and he is surveying the nations for hearts that long to be connected to him in a powerful way. Heaven is our home and the Holy Spirit nestled in with the word of God is our access point to experience and live from heaven to earth. Jesus wants us closer always closer.

Michael Koulianos talks about this in his book 'Holy Spirit: The one who makes Jesus real.' his times of intimacy with the Holy Spirit are a continuous rhythm of his life. The adventures that are released in this context are extraordinary. These times of closeness are often unseen to the natural eye but bliss to the person who makes Jesus their pinnacle explorative duty in this life. That's what life was and is meant to be lived for. Him, only him.

Simplicity in the kingdom is paramount. We are never stuck inside of his will, never out of ideas. He is releasing fresh mercies daily. Daily portions of grace, breakthrough and blessing belong to him. they are his and that is our normal. Nothing else matters apart from him, he dresses us. He makes us whole.

Chapter 10

Replace lies with truth

Lies never surrender but they do fall silent and collapse under the superior weight of truth. Adolf Hitler in World War 2 groomed a nation as his cult. His ideology was backed with philosophy and science rooted in the occult. his lies were surrounding his heart birthing passion. His response was to capture Europe for himself, greed gave way to deception and deception gave way to genocide, E.M Bonds says that "prayer will sweep enemies out of the way." A nice phrase but prayer without action is like a business that is open, has staff on their payroll in their shop but there are no cutting-edge products that are in demand by consumers, we need to work the prayers that God gives us.

Silence is okay in context but it is not okay in wartime, it is detrimental in fact. Prayer is the lubricant, the oil, the fuel, our corresponding actions are the motor, the engine and when we press the accelerator, we are in a strong place in God to take down enemies that entrap us from realizing the fullness of our potential in Christ. There is no limit to what we can achieve in him, only 'in Christ' are there A plus's with no blemishes on the answers, every answer is within reach to solve our life's exam.

Prophecy gives vision but our heart is stirred when we begin making tangible moves forward in the direction of the prophetic promises that God gives us. God's promises are everlasting but our lack of agreement with the Lord at times stunts the full effects of our destinies or propels us backward with fresh winds of his grace and hope absent. Bowing to fear is the opposite of being obedient to hope and hope never disappoints when it is grounded in God's word. The enemy feeds off doom and gloom, he is not going to bring us into fresh avenues of grace and hope if we are shut off from his direction and the leadership of the Holy Spirit.

When i'm making sacrifices of time for a greater purpose, my exploits will either be blessed or cursed depending on what version of the spiritual realm that I agree with. Agreeing with Jesus and capturing the thoughts of heaven is a powerful way to change your life for the better and to grant access to new doors of opportunity and drink from the fountain of breakthrough. God is in the blessing business. Satan has struggles to beat you down and devalue you. Christ will have none of this, he is also in the restoration business. There is nothing good outside of his will and there is nothing problematic inside of your current circumstance that he doesn't have the equipment to fix and restore. If you have felt broken, beat down or discouraged, Doctor Jesus is merely an opening conversation away. He can aid and help to bring a fresh lease of life, mission and wisdom where there has been lack. Control is the antithesis of trust and Jesus desires that we trust him because he is good and he is true to his word.

To walk in freedom from control there has to be a letting go of control. Control is witchcraft, it is burdensome, it is not fun to operate on a witchcraft basis, it is thinking elevated above the realm of Godly intelligence. Pride lifts up self and man. God lifts up the other members of the trinity, he points to their wonder and they all work together as one unit. God is not disoriented in his triune identity. He is fully immersed and comfortable in his identity as God and ruler of the universe. Michael J Norton says that "Anything that is worshiped other than God is demonic" How true! Entertainment and the flesh lifted up above the purity that is found in a loving and life sustaining connection with the God of the universe is a trap. I'm speaking to myself here but how often do we as his beloved shy away from the secret place to get the information and revelation that we need to usher in the blessings of God?

Chapter 11

Produce work that makes your heart sing

The art we produce is longing, crying out to be graced with Jesus signature. From the flowers in our gardens to the music that we play and the people that we associate with. This is all crying out for Jesus. Jesus alone can install within us his creative best. So many films in Hollywood are infused with creative genius, real grunt, I admire the storytellers with a very real story telling and operative gift like Guy Ritchie and Quentin Tarantino. I admire their knack for beautiful dialogue and music that builds depth to their scenes and characters. Although many of the storylines are woven with heavy violence, immorality and foul language I can still recognize and congratulate the gifting that is evident over their lives. To balance off the above statement I do urge you to turn away from violent material as much as possible so in no way am I validating that part of their art and I do urge you not to view scenes that would stir up the flesh in an unhealthy way.

We all have sneaky giftings waiting to be discovered, brought to the surface and polished for everyday usage. This is the privilege we get as humanity to realise our potential in this life. Giftings are nonexclusive to God loyalty. You can use your God breathed talents for good or for evil depending on where you sit on the issue of who or what God is to you. Gifts require time to become excellent at but they are entirely worth it. They are significant on your path to joy and wholeness. In chariots of fire the main actor says that when he runs he 'feels Gods pleasure.' I can relate, in the game of cricket as a batter when in form and batting beautifully it felt easy, restful, rhythmic, like I was painting with willow and my eyes and body were picking up the deft touches of a novel written by King or the brushstrokes of a Picasso painting. I felt good in that setting and I know that when in form God was delighting in my skills too. Our gifts are longing for his grace and our co-operation

Jesus through the victory of the cross washes us daily with fresh avenues and pathways of hope. 'Hope is the anchor for the soul.' This means you are commanded and invited to solidify your vision for life laced with hope. There is no setback in your life that the cross did not overcome and reign victories over. Jesus is not slinking back under the weight of the nails on the cross, he instead rose victorious.

When you start altering and tinkering with God's best for your life it sets up difficulty. I know for me the flesh is defeated on the cross, but my life message is one of anchored belief in the promises of God and stepping into our corporate and individual promised land. Prosperity is not stuff; absent of personal responsibility, it is beauty and joy connected to the goodness of God. Prosperity when it is viewed correctly is not an idol but a place that we rest and delight in.

Chapter 12

Pray and pray again...

Digging into realms of prayer is seen as a lost art. Prayer unlocks blessings. Prayerlessness always creates lack, carnal expressions and lifestyles that contradict and chuck mud at the fullness of Jesus life and teachings. Fullness is what Jesus came to give us not pain and sorrow. Sometimes we have to go through things that are not ideal or fun but with Christ in us, he is Jesus the hope of the world.

When you're feeling low, the right thing to do is not to beat yourself up it is a time to meditate on the promises of God. The promises of God are timeless. They are for today, tomorrow and the next day. They carry us forward and propel us all into unchartered territory. I love it when God brings me out of personal funks that i get myself into by not syncing with Gods rhythm. Its God's gentleness that we need to catapault us forward.

Confusion, doubt, unbelief - none of that cognitive diffusion is from God's Kingdom. None of it. When we passionately pursue God's best he is more than ready to lavish us with his best. That's the power of the cross and the goodness of God.

Chapter 13

Expand your heart's vision?! Expand your life!

God is a mastermind of expansion. Lack and obscurity is not found with him. These are tools of the demonic. Christ in us, shepherds us from the effects of evil. Christ in us truly is the hope of all glory. when there are struggles, Christ is present to deliver us fully from these troubles with the delicacy of an experienced knitter or the delicate brushstrokes of an artist that specializes in realism.

God releases us as we learn to abide in him, giving over our own ideas of what is right and being guided by his love. It's a beautiful reality to know that God wants us to overcome, he champions our growth, sustains us in dark times and lavishes upon us fresh realms of his mercy and grace each and every day. Poverty and sickness are not from him, they are demonic in origin and they need to be treated as such. The line that governments had and have taken on the Coronavirus pandemic has been off target to the Lord's will, puffing up science and fear is not from heaven's playbook, the fathers heart is grieving over the nations strategies that have shoved moral truth to the backbenches. Gratitude and living immersed in God's promises is a firm tactic to get nations out of the pickle that they are in. Debt and borrowing are the norm right now, when you don't have answers on this level it's a little bit like Ben Stiller's character in the film Dodgeball who gives up, begins eating Fast food non-stop, gains weight and blames Chuck Norris for his downfall.

We can't as believers sink to the depths of the ocean like the Titanic when we are designed to soar like eagles across fresh terrain and ascend spectacular heights. Love and truth are the answer, they always are and always will be. We can't progress as people and nations without these weapons operating at their maximum voltage in our hearts and minds. The mind and the heart operating in unison is a powerful force indeed.

God will waste no time in putting the furniture of life in order to beautify your surroundings when you have a heart to know him, a ministry to love him. Love conquers in the darkest of places. The love of Christ is catalytic in tearing down the forces of darkness that ravage our hearts, cities, nations and international communities. Darkness is the lonesome road that never gets brighter.

Truth shepherds us in a mountain of fear. Fear sells newspapers and it closes up hearts to the truth. The truth when it resonates in our hearts like the delicate hushed tones of a melody gives way to courage so that we can shift gears and revitalize our surroundings with an outpouring of fresh projects and products, true pursuits that make a difference, outputs that hold eternal and practical importance. Truth and peace are unfathomable to the mind that is in a rut with only the world's agenda as their pseudo anchor. Christ in us shakes out our deficits, hang ups, poison and betrayal. He wants us to live blessed and in abundance, his debit card isn't declining, his vegetables aren't becoming rotten.

He is the God of today, we just have to know this instinctively from our depths. His muscle is unlimited for tackling the issues that hurt us. The issues of career, health, family, finances, and governments are not beyond heavens reach. God is patient but his 'truth is marching on.' He is so loving, and kind. He won't lead us astray or punish us beyond repair. He has a helping hand with fresh hope ready to be released.

Chapter 14

Develop your talents

Talent is too often relegated to the sidelines of our lives as we pursue careers and families, doing the stuff without really taking the time to acknowledge God and protect ourselves from burnout. Burnout is a very real phenomenon and it is accessed by not honouring God with the biblical commandment to rest. A rested mind is a creative mind that can see into inspiring and never ending passageways of revelation. Heaven will continue to unpack gems of insight into eternity.

Insight is dug out through hard yards of time spent chewing on the scriptures and delighting in his presence but it is also found in the nuances of peace and rest. Take for example two adolescents in love on the ground looking up at the sky where there are clouds. After a few moments the clouds no longer look like fluffy white Samoyeds without eyes but they take shape, they look like dinosaurs and ships. The creative mind begin to be engaged. Stories begin to evolve, laughter fills the air, the heart is awakened and joy is released. Creative expression that is fresh and vibrant is actually a unique and fun evangelistic tool for the lost. Jesus wants to be let loose to reign free and breathe life into our creative expression. Our creativity is no longer confined to the edges of our lives or seen within the context of a secular and sacred divide.

Jesus wants to be involved and release creative expression in the arts, governance and sports, every facet of society is longing for heaven to dress it with royal robes and panache but it can only be founded in developing a close-knit interconnected relationship with the creator. Two-way connection with the Lord is indeed producing an output whereby the kingdom of God is being built into the fabric of society.

Chapter 15

Prioritise your relationship to God and let joy flow!

It's the overflow of relationship with God that God blesses and enlarges your perspective of life. We get big on the inside in our spirit man and then we attack the issues of life that are besetting culture as we see them with the grace of God and our rich connection with the Holy Spirit that is elasticized by being engrossed in the scriptures, we need to build a solid worldview from the scriptures. The scriptures are nourishment for the soul. They are life, they are a lived reality. We breathe in his words and then we exhale to the world around us his victory song.

Joy in the Kingdom is awesome, Satan can throw out a counterfeit but when the Holy Spirit releases joy it is often accompanied with corresponding fruit, if you want to know if it's authentic just do a fruit check. Simple. I've experienced Holy Spirit laughter it's awesome, best tonic on the market and it's entirely free, just check the fruit people.

Religion is toxic, my heart and mind agrees with that statement wholeheartedly and we need to be aware of the tactics of religion that overemphasize laws at the expense of our connection to the Father, son and Holy Spirit, it is in essence form without power, it is striving rather than excellence, it's drudgery, it's toxic. If you study Jesus life and teachings he was known as the 'friend of sinners' so he didn't suck up to the elite or religious hierarchy, he was on a mission. In essence he was a revolutionary, he gave context to the world around him through his life of love and questioned the status quo, he was curious and powerful with thousands of miracles documented and millions more after his death, burial and resurrection. He was and is the saviour and King of the universe, King Jesus.

FIN

SALVATION PRAYER

If after reading Power thought 4 Christians you would like to become a Christian and commence a friendship with Jesus initiating a brand-new adventure with him at the centre of your life, leading and guiding you please pray this prayer:

'Lord Jesus, I've mucked up too many times to count but today is a new day and I choose you to be my bestie and saviour. I trust you to take care of all the garbage of my past that hurt people, hurt you and hurt me through your son Jesus Christ who I believe died on the cross for my mishaps, blunders and shame. I choose a new path and welcome the Father, Son and Holy Spirit to be God of my life from this moment forward. I choose to turn from my sins completely with your grace helping me to live a brand-new way with you as Lord of my life. I invite the Holy Spirit to live inside of me, revealing Jesus more and more and fill me to overflowing with your gifts, character and abiding presence. I release this prayer to you in faith in the name of the Father, Son and Holy Spirit. Amen.'

If you have prayed that prayer, AMAZING! welcome to your new Christian family and righteous identity in Christ! From here?! Please attend a Christian Bible based church in your local area that welcomes the Father, Son and Holy

Spirit and experience the world of the Bible in your day-to-day life like never before!

ABOUT THE AUTHOR

Callum Coker is a Christian who is passionate about pursuing the Holy Spirit, connecting people to Jesus in the context that they live in and seeing this planet become the 'Heaven on Earth' reality that is available for individuals, communities and nations. He is the author of 'THE FREEDOM MESSAGE', a series of books that reimagines the world of the Bible within the context of the 21st Century. He has a passion for creativity and imagination whilst holding close the pillars of sound theology and artistic expression through his work. Callum likes sports, reading and playing guitar. When he's not doing these recreational pursuits, he likes to spend time with friends, family and work on his next project, whatever that may be.

www.ingramcontent.com/pod-product-compliance
Lightning Source LLC
Chambersburg PA
CBHW070041070426
42449CB00012BA/3125